By the same author
TIGER TREK

WHEN THE RIVERS GO HOME

WRITTEN AND ILLUSTRATED BY TED LEWIN

Macmillan Publishing Company   New York
Maxwell Macmillan Canada   Toronto
Maxwell Macmillan International   New York   Oxford   Singapore   Sydney

Macmillan Publishing Company
866 Third Avenue
New York, NY 10022
Maxwell Macmillan Canada, Inc.
1200 Eglinton Avenue East
Suite 200
Don Mills, Ontario M3C 3N1
First edition
Printed in Hong Kong
10   9   8   7   6   5   4   3   2   1
The text of this book is set in 14 point Trump Medieval.
The illustrations are rendered in watercolor on paper.
Library of Congress Cataloging-in-Publication Data
Lewin, Ted.
    When the rivers go home / written and illustrated by Ted Lewin. — 1st ed.
        p.   cm.
    Summary: Describes life in the marsh in Brazil known as the Pantanal.
    ISBN 0-02-757382-6
    1. Marsh ecology—Brazil—Pantanal—Juvenile literature.   2. Marsh
fauna—Brazil—Pantanal—Juvenile literature.   3. Marsh flora—
Brazil—Pantanal—Juvenile literature.   [1. Marsh ecology—Brazil.
2. Ecology—Brazil.]   I. Title.
QH117.L58   1992
508.81′71—dc20   90-19937

INTRODUCTION

In Brazil, in the almost exact center of South America, there is a marsh the size of Pennsylvania. It's called *Pantanal*, which means "big swamp" in Portuguese. In the wet season the rivers overflow their banks, flooding the plains and making islands of the forest patches. In the dry season countless ponds and streams left by the receding waters trap millions of fish. Birds and other wild creatures gather in huge numbers to feast on this windfall and, sometimes, on each other.

There is a dusty, arrow-straight road through the heart of the Pantanal. It is eighty-five bumpy miles long, and crosses more than one hundred rough wooden bridges. Along it you can see more South American caiman, or *jacare*, than you thought possible: Jacare piled on jacare. Jacare crawling over jacare. Birds tiptoeing between jacare. Cattle stepping over jacare. Jacare eating piranhas. Piranhas eating jacare. There are rodents big enough to saddle, birds that scream, and snakes as long as limousines. On the ranches, or *fazendas*, along its length, cowboys as tough as shoe leather herd cattle, cracking their fifteen-foot-long bullwhips like lightning bolts. The ponies they ride can close their nostrils while grazing on underwater grass.

In the streams and rivers, *Pantaneiros*, the people of the Pantanal, sit still as herons in hollowed-out logs, fishing with pole or bow and arrow. Along the banks and stream edges, toothy jacare fish in their own ancient way, while in the jungle beyond, howler monkeys shake the treetops and roar like lions in a hurricane. All this harmony is under serious threat from the outside. Mercury pollution from gold mining, pesticides from soybean farming, deforestation for agriculture, and poaching all need to be reconciled with the preservation of this natural wonder.

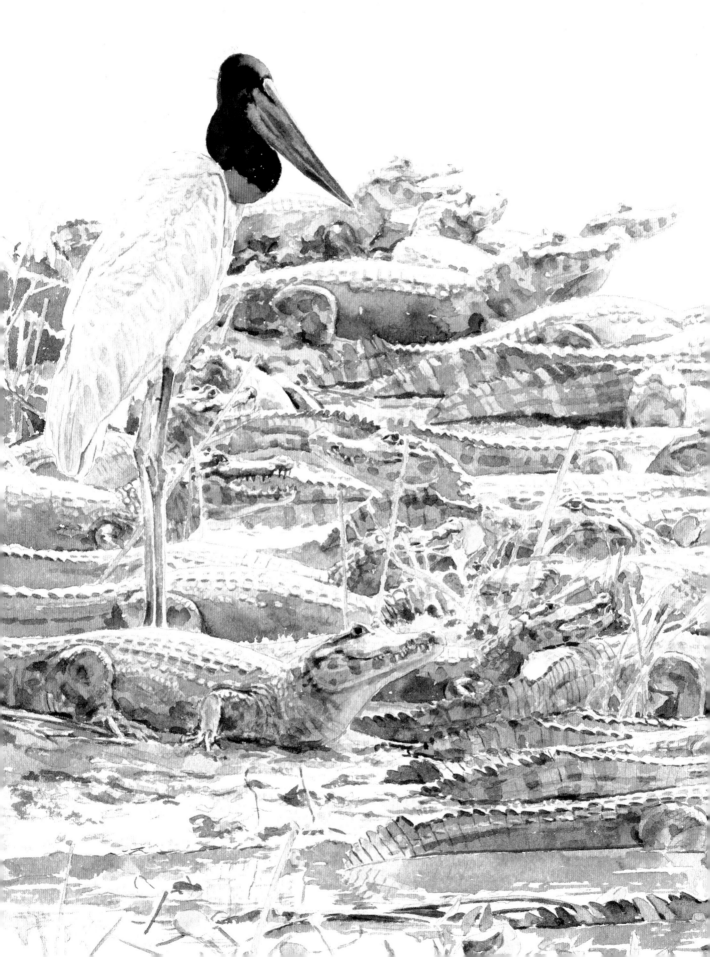

On either side of the road as far as the eye can see, logjams of jacare clog the streams and ponds. Jabiru storks feed among them in the shallows.

Grazing cattle step gingerly over the jacare. Neither the cattle nor the jabiru have anything to fear from the sharp teeth; jacare prefer fish.

Nearby, a pair of chicken-like Southern screamers take time off from their screaming for a cool drink.

Scanning the pond below, a snail kite watches for his favorite food, the apple snail. The kite will snatch it from the water with his talons and, with his very special beak, remove it from its shell.

The water in another pond boils like a hot sulphur spring—with fish. A splashing, and a crunching of bone and scale…jacare are feeding on fish trapped in the dying pond.

One youngster has caught a pintaro. He flees to a high bank where he and his prize will be safe from bigger, hungry jaws.

A Pantaneiro family in a dugout canoe fishes for piranhas at a quiet spot in the river.

A capped heron has already caught one and rests nearby.

Farther downriver a sound like a thousand cranky babies and the powerful smell of fish and bird— the enchanted land of a *vivaro*, or bird rookery. Thousands of nesting birds: spoonbills, woodstorks, egrets, herons. When feeding regurgitated fish to their chicks, the parents sometimes miss the mark, and it rains fish below.

A spoonbill chick has fallen out of the nest and broken its legs. It lies spreadwinged and helpless on the water hyacinth like an exotic lady's fan, its bill making soft thwacks like wood covered in velvet. It will not last the day.

Later, along the road a *capybara*, the largest rodent in the world, wallows in glue-like mud to cool off and to rid itself of pests. He looks like a furry little hippo. Mud drips from his chin. He hears something, snorts, and gallops away.

A cloud of golden dust rises on the road. Shouting, and the crack of bullwhips—*vaqueiros*, the cowboys of the Pantanal, on a cattle drive!

Hundreds of pale, lean, humpbacked cattle squeeze by on the narrow road, urged on by the shouts and whistles of the Vaqueiros.

Wirey men on wirey ponies and mules keep the cattle up on the road.

Very quickly the herd is past, and fades again into the dust.

It is late afternoon and we have reached the end of the road. Hyacinth macaws in a flash of blue land, shrieking, in the topmost tree branches. They are the largest, most spectacular, and noisiest parrots in the world—and quickly becoming one of the rarest.

Soon the rains will come and the rivers will overflow
their banks. The cattle will head for high ground,
and the birds and animals disappear into the vast
tranquility of their drowned land.